American Patriotism

This book is for the future of America — our children.
The author of this book hopes that the book
will be read to children all across this great land,
and that those who read it will engage in dialogue
that far exceeds the writing on these pages.

by Kerry Patton
Illustrations by Rachel Simmons

Stand Up America Publishing

American

Library of Congress Cataloging-in-Publication Data

Patton, Kerry.

American Patriotism / written by Kerry Patton and illustrated by Rachel Simmons

Summary: Defines what American Patriotism means and gives examples of what
it looks like in our everyday lives.

ISBN:978-0615457697

[1. Patriotism—Juvenile literature. 2. Citizenship—Juvenile literature. 3. Alphabet letters]

I. Simmons, Rachel, ill.   II. Title.

© 2011 Stand Up America Publishing

For information regarding permission, write to:

Stand Up America Publishing
P.O. Box 1596, Bigfork, MT 59911

Printed in the U.S.A.

Patriotism

"There is no better time in our history as Americans
to bond together as family to discuss our history and Constitution
as well as our patriotic duties and responsibilities.
In this book, Patton and Simmons have created a foundation
of morals and values which should be instilled in the heart of every
American —especially our children, who are the future of our nation.
This book serves well as the first step in bringing family together
to discuss such important aspects of being ambassadors
to the rest of the world and our own communities."

Paul E. Vallely
Chairman Stand Up America
www.standupamericaus.com

American

Patriotism

Acknowledgements:

Without the following individuals, this book could never have been created: Major General Paul Vallely (Army Ret.), you have been nothing but a true mentor throughout the majority of my professional career, and for that alone I cannot thank you enough. Heidi Roedel and Kathleen Hawkins have an eye for perfection. Without them and their attention to detail, this book would have been a complete disaster.

While those mentioned above are deserving of praise, none deserves as much gratitude as one very young, especially talented woman named Rachel Simmons. Rachel is an exceptional artist who is able to translate ideas into meaningful pictures that truly convey the intended message, a difficult challenge for even the most seasoned artist. Rachel, you truly are an American Patriot, and I, along with your friends and family, could not be more proud of you. Lastly, on behalf of every person involved in the creation of this book, we all would like to thank God for the continuous strength, courage, and wisdom provided to keep this great nation truly the best place on earth.

American

The United States of America

Patriotism

America is the land of the free.

Patriotism

Men and women have died for our freedoms;
never forget them in your prayers.

AmErican

Patriotism

Equality means all men and women
are created equal and should
have equal opportunities.
What you do with your opportunities
will determine your greatness.

Patriotism

Represent yourself to the world as an American who is willing to voluntarily serve those in need.

Patriotism

Independence means that we will
never rely on anyone other than
our fellow Americans.

AmeriCan

Declaration of Independence

The United States Constitution

Bill of Rights

Patriotism

Charters of freedom such as the
U.S. Constitution,
the ***Declaration of Independence***,
and the ***Bill of Rights***
should be the documents you live by;
they protect your rights and privileges
and make America the greatest place to live.

Patriotism

A lot of people may not like you
because you are an American.
These people do not have the same freedoms
as you do, like the freedom to
choose what you want to be when you grow up,
who you want to be friends with,
and where you want to go.
The best thing you can do for these people
is to show them good will, generosity,
and kindness.
Then they will see that
Americans are beautiful people.

AmericaN

Patriotism

Never hesitate to stand up for what you believe in.
You are an American; you have freedom of speech,
expression, religion, and many other
wonderful freedoms that people
in other countries do not enjoy.
Use them and show the world who you are.

Patriotism

Pledge allegiance to the American flag
with respect and dignity.
Stand still and place your right hand over your heart.
If you're wearing a hat, take it off.
Think about the words and what they mean.
Live the rest of your day remembering those words.

PAtriotism

Appreciate everything you have in life.
Many people living in this world
are not as fortunate as you are.

American

PaTriotism

Treat others as you would like to be treated.
An American Patriot who treats others
with kindness and respect
will give them hope and set a good example.

American

PatRiotism

Respect those who think differently than you do.
Americans don't have to agree on everything
to get along and work together.

PatrIotism

In God We Trust.
That is the American motto.
Live by it, have faith in God,
and never forget Him.

American

PatriOtism

Obligate yourself to tell someone
"I love you" at least once a day.
Say it to someone you care about.
Say it to someone who needs strength.
Love is strong, and the love you will find
among those who have served the United States
is some of the strongest love there is.

American

PatrioTism

Truth is difficult to accept.
The world is filled with lies.
Seek the truth and spread
your knowledge wisely.

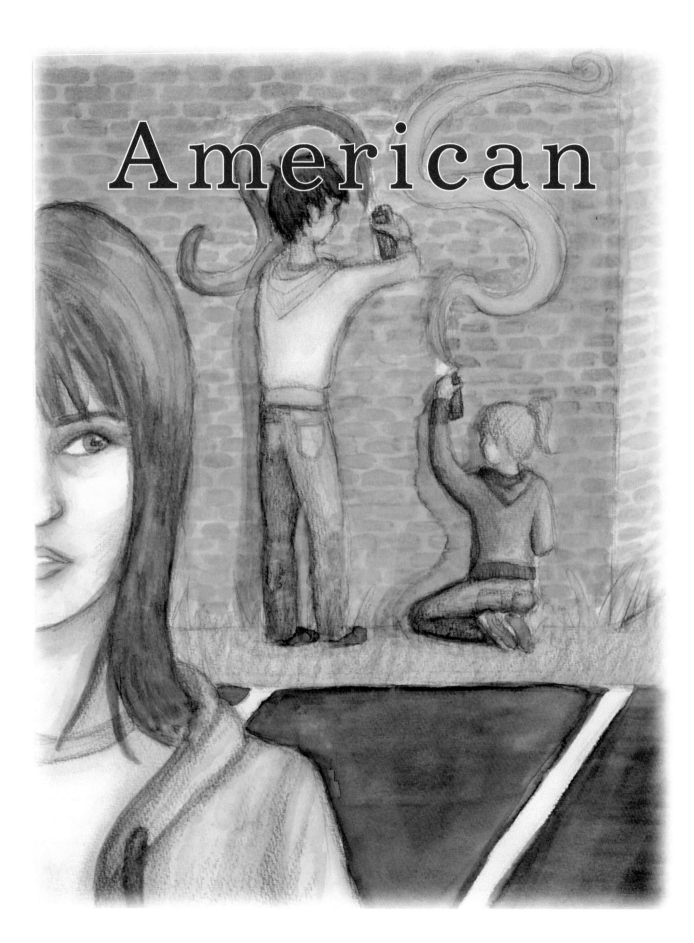

Patriot**I**sm

Individualism means that you are special.
No one else is quite like you.
Don't let others pressure you into doing things
that aren't right.
America is not a land of conformists.
Fight for what you believe in
and remain true to yourself.

American

PatriotiSm

Sacrifice.
Give that which you hold dear and close to you.
Men and women paid
the ultimate sacrifice for all Americans.
There is no better gift than that
which you are willing to sacrifice.

American

PatriotisM

Mercy should be engrained in your heart
and soul even for those who appear
to be doing wrong.
Be compassionate to all and you will find
others doing the same.

AMERICAN

PATRIOT

Being an **American Patriot** is not easy.
You will find challenges and temptations
throughout your life.
Stick to these principles,
and you will be a truly
wonderful **American Patriot.**

The definition of "patriotism"
according to the
Webster Dictionary of 1848.

"Love of one's country; the passion which aims
to serve one's country, either in defending it from invasion,
or protecting its rights and maintaining
its laws and institutions in vigor and purity.
Patriotism is the characteristic of a good citizen,
the noblest passion that animates a man in the
character of a citizen."

AUTHOR

Kerry Patton served in the U.S. Departments of Justice and Defense and as a contractor within the Homeland Security and State Departments. He has worked in South America, Africa, the Middle East, Asia and Europe, focusing on security and intelligence, and has interviewed current and former terrorists, including members of the Taliban. He is the author of "Sociocultural Intelligence: The New Discipline of Intelligence Studies." Currently Mr. Patton teaches for Henley Putnam University and is the Northeast Regional Director for Stand Up America.

Rachel Simmons is a recent inductee into the National Honors Society. A true artist at heart, Rachel is an avid pianist and guitarist. She is passionate about the world in which we live, hoping to one day travel extensively helping those in need. Most importantly, Rachel is committed to assisting our veterans and their family members. Eventually, Rachel would like to pursue a career in which she can positively influence others using her artistic abilities.

ILLUSTRATOR